P9-AFW-456

WITHDRAWN
UTSA LIBRARIES

DESIRE
Poems 1978-1982

Jody Aliesan

books by Jody Aliesan:

Soul Claiming

as if it will matter

Desire

Thanks to the editors of the following journals, where some of these poems were first published: *Berkeley Poets Cooperative, Calyx, Image* (with award from Seattle Arts Commission), *Negative Capability, Northwest Passage, Quarry West* (University of California at Santa Cruz), *Remedy* (Physicians for Social Responsibility), *Studia Mystica* (California State University at Sacramento), *Tilth, Yellow Silk,* and the University of Washington YWCA *Newsletter.*

"letter" first appeared in *Pioneer Letters: the Letter as Literature,* published by Northwest Review Books, 1980.

"spell" was included in a broadside series by Jawbone Press, 1982.

"laboratory report" became part of a collaborative piece with sculptor Phillip Schwab which was selected for the Tacoma Art Museum's 10th Annual Painting and Sculpture Exhibition (1981), Tacoma, Washington, and exhibited subsequently in his two-person show at the same museum (1982).

"horror vacui" also developed into a collaborative piece with Phillip Schwab and was included in the two-person show at the Tacoma Art Museum (1982).

"desire" and "angelus" were illustrated by Fred Birchman in drawings, the first included in "Pacific Northwest Drawing Perspectives," a traveling exhibition (1982) and the second in solo exhibitions at the Francine Seders Gallery, Seattle and the Western Gallery, Western Washington State University, Bellingham.

copyright © 1985 Jody Aliesan

LIBRARY
The University of Texas
At San Antonio

EMPTY BOWL   P.O. 646   Port Townsend WA. 98368

for Phillip

who sees me
through

Contents

argument

summoned from silence
into the fever of voices
which one is mine

I said all I had to say no one
was listening we haven't much
time left there are more important
things to be doing leave me alone

>   *slice your brain with a razor*
>   *make distinctions   this*
>   *is not exactly that*

sometimes I think I know what's true
other times I have no idea what's real
carpenter ants empty my head
mouthful by mouthful
only bats flutter
between these trees

>   *put your ear to the wood*
>   *you can hear it burning   find*
>   *the wide bellycurve of the sea*

the signals come too quickly
wave bands wave trains rough wind chop
seiches and breakers surfbeat uprush
shuffle slide and sprawl up across
the face of the beach towing back
rippling into frequencies

listen to the long low swells
tsunamis with news of volcanoes

the signals overlap
stations slide together on the dial
how far away are you
do you still exist

I can't be figured out
just experience me

I've got to surrender
to the power of it
surrender to the power

everything
is so beautiful why
do we make it hard

DESIRE

desire

on a bridge over fish ladders
I watch down five weirs
for one of the dark-backed coho
salmon I saw jumping outside

waiting for its tail-writhe splatter shiny
climb up the small falls waiting

mostly for the glide
afterwards   wet
slide over the wall's lip
sigh into the next pool's swallow

one comes now
firm-muscled tensely
slippery up toward me
trembling and urgent

I loosen to accept and close around
my own flesh memory:
sea smell rises with the spawn-fish spasm

or is it mine

spell

let the woodworker's hands broad and smooth
twining veins on a lattice of tendons
lift your leg like the neck of a cello

let the one who strokes feathers from paper
with the brush of his fingertips draw
your lips and the nipple of your fiercest

       quickening you must
       press his face away his
       slightest breathing is
       too much to bear

let the sculptor's hands burnish and strew
your bronze sand into the furnace
ground oyster shell fanned under birds

fall down on the field-quilted waters
his bone-nosed eagle his knee-bent
stallion his hanging fish will find you

conversation

I was a passionate nun I still am
now I satisfy the passion
it's one thing finding pleasure in virtue
another finding pleasure in pleasure
being a nun has nothing to do with
chastity it has to do
with a lantern in the head

keeping that light needs earthly fuel
not only good fruit and bread
but the milk of our flesh
I need to stand by
when she goes off like this
laser firefly alone in the dark

the book about amish quilts
spoke of frustration
how intense purple patchwork
shiny swept wooden floors
brilliant gardens released
expression of desire
for wholeness union

also the kind that rides
between the thighs from wine
of wide open eyes each of us
looking into the other's downy mineshaft
recognizing the expression in that mirror
when we come

still the devotion essence of simple tasks
precision and care for its own sake

the cell lined with comforters

still sacred manner of soul's incandescence

also matter spiraling in spasms
along the silky side

holdup

when the man who walked up to the open window
of your pickup truck to ask directions just
as you were easing out of the tight parking space
changes his tone of voice and pushes
a dirty automatic into your lover's neck

> *give me everything*
> *or I'll blow your head off*

all the rest is clear and slow invisible snow
drifts around your body into your mind
only later will you think of all the moves
you could have made   the words that might
have worked but nothing is clearer than submitting

> *give me everything*

even then   even after the looking back
and the next days you see it over again
and again   the walk up closer the flash of metal
the rush of what you didn't let yourself
feel that night when you both said afterwards we're

> *or I'll blow your head off*

all right we're liars to say so but this
is what we have to do now   later we'll
curl up in one another's lap   later
we'll stand each separate in the long cold wind
where no one can help you feel any less alone

admit you don't know how to live

any racking of your spheres
is scattered by a new particle
a windup from the great pitcher
delivered so cleanly the wood splits
end to end

two leathery-winged deaf pelted
animalbirds scutter into a crevice

just when you've programmed the set
memorized fresh lines in your
commonplace book
                the cue comes
at an arbitrary place in the dialogue

prompt screens go blank the actors
stare back at the audience

turn wide-eyed off the rain-dark
backwoods road to a cellar light
down stairs door to a meeting hall

excuse me I'm lost

wooden folding chairs stutter
whiteshirt bald heads shine
as the bible class rises to save you

valentine's day

a young woman stands in a parlor
pulling a wedding dress on over her head
it is a wedding dress too short
and tight in the arms

> *each time she dreams*
> *the church is a corridor*
> *the walls closing in*
> *along the aisle until*

a large older woman enters
from the next room and says yes
that's fine   the older woman exits

voices in the next room
speak again of the memorial
they will present in church that morning
for the older woman's mother
the young woman's grandmother
who died a year ago

> *there is room only*
> *for carnival booths*
> *selling wedding rings*

the young woman lifts a long veil
out of a box begins to fit it
on her head   the older woman
enters again and takes it from her
shows her how to place it so the weight

of the cloth won't pull it off
the older woman nods and leaves

> *the cheapest by the door*
> *the most expensive*
> *near the altar*

the young woman stands quietly
looking out the parlor windows
she opens the door and moves
out of the shadowed room into the day
down the street toward a white
clapboard church where children play
in the worn grass courtyard

> *she and the man stop*
> *halfway down the aisle*
> *to choose a ring*
> *she has not yet seen*
> *the man's face*

she climbs the back steps
opens the church door
it is a stage door it faces
rows of people they are now
stirring and gasping

> *when they reach the altar*
> *the minister has no head*

18

a man in the front row holds up
a death's head made of straw
the young woman remembers she is
not supposed to be seen before the wedding
the death's head is an old custom
the man holding it is surprised to fulfill
she closes the door and runs down the steps
across the beaten grass
to an eroded path

> *each time after the wedding*
> *she is led onto a grassy mound*
> *the dress frays at the hem*
> *the veil is torn*

people turn to stare at her
children in the midst of their game
a policeman standing ahead on the path
offers his arm
she feels a tug on her veil a cat
a robust dark cat has snatched it
as she dragged it past
she reaches down to unhook the claw
on the front steps of the church
people are gathering

> *each time she breaks loose*
> *runs down a long hill*
> *leaping over bodies of lovers*
> *lying in the grass*

she hides behind the building
where the foundation is bare
through wooden piers and pilings
she watches legs and feet
arrive and mill about

> *when she reaches the bottom*
> *she spreads her arms wide*

> *from behind hands grab her wrists*
> *she is led up the hill*
> *to be married again*

a hand pulls heavy down on her shoulder
it is one of the older women
carrying the music they will sing

> *the last time she dreamed it*
> *she looked at the dress it was*
> *scarlet satin and black lace*

the older woman says it was nice of you
to allow the memorial
in the middle of your wedding
the young woman says it's all right
the older woman says you were asked
weren't you

the young woman
looks away she says
it's all right

end of eleven years

you've learned how to survive
but there's no need for survival
what is it you want to inherit

alder trees as I move through them
finger the winter sun among
their twigs dividing plain sky
windows into facets glittering

I sift their ashes for the garden
sick of routine round decay renewal
ash settles into my hair too soon
to throw the shovel down

and run from signs of dying even
signs of birth its disappointment
this warm spell fooled
grape hyacinth shoots they'll burn

in the next frost paper embryos
of birds flake on the pavement
with the coming of spring

                    *

as we grow older
our choices are more between goods

with fate on the lee side first free will
then living with what's left no mistakes

only consequences the choices
never wholly made who knows these ashes

may flash again burnished feathers
fly us back to the trees

*

on top of the hill a woman winds
gray metal mechanical dove smooths
hands around shiny shoulders wings
her fingertips under its breast gently

swings it up into hingeflapping fall
clattering coasted glide to the grass
she waits it doesn't move

she walks down kneels and slides
its steel up onto her palms she does this
over and over while all around
live swallows scream pendulums

may day (with thanks to H.G. Wells)

being a perfectionist and being scared
are often the same thing

—*John Fowles*

I crash through brambles every time
into the same clearing
someone hold me stroke me rock me
until I fall asleep until morning

god has no thighs when I cry
out to him in the night
he doesn't turn over and ask
is something the matter

wild animals give everything to fate
but they still move away from what hurts

before it scalds hot water feels cool
only when sweat rushes from organs to skin
do I reel blind throw up
hands eyes wade into the sound
without stopping prairie child
never seen anything taller than creeks
thrown into deep end swimming pool
life erupting in green chlorine bubbles

after we saw whales she asked *did you cry*
as I get older I cry more easily

every spring clawing up cedar roots
hacking back ivy blackberry vines
they want to take over I'm tired
of struggling I want someone to tell me
what's best for me I feel like giving up

wonderful she said *that's progress*
how long can this go on
don't lose your nerve

horror vacui

forgive me . . . but I have to hold hand
over mouth in order to keep quiet

Federico Garcia Lorca

these seem real:
the clarity of disaster
the rush up of death's frontal mask
the daily small deaths of belief
setting all in order setting off heartflesh
in a sheath-shroud of cool high blue-white noise
a knife to the bone

frantic in crowded pools
pulled up dripping on the edge of the tank
everyone else easy
in the element of drowning
how to swim again
whether to want joining
that school of no questions

faraway steely eyes mirror yours
not in anguish but pregnant with knowing
full term with suppressed tears
living under a shadow
we must open them wide
hands each in the other's lap
can the jump of that spark
shock us back into life

yes

claustrophobic death in life
choked sleepwalk through rooms
overheated by safety
pace of watchspring habit
easy bath stagnant with steam
lungs scream get me out of here
iron rusts the web unravels
wood rots flesh sags
it's time to leave for loneliness

on the night open rockplain
stinging rain tightens my face
wraps my hide closer around bones
alert in cool lairs I await
the draped woman who walks luminous
cask in hand *do you know*
what I carry she asks
this is yours if you name it

some of us meet pain by feeling it
I said   others by not
the rest by giving it meaning
I quarrel with holiness yes
desire causes suffering
and to give up desire eases ache
but who wants to live without desire
we are not sent to this world for doing
what we can't put our hearts into

she said *you are cursed to sing*
only one part of the fugue you hear
cursed more to believe someone else
also knows the house is burning
also knows the way
to the grove and the pit sings
another weft over deep ostinato
another shiny wire railing
despite the edge whose eyes
are as old as yours and as dumb
with passion no it won't last

nothing does but why miss it

song

with the best lovers
we are always virgin
the old woman said
herself fresh-turned
in the rolling bed

this is what the angels envy us for
they may have everything they need
but not all the needs
they could like

the world may not make sense
but it's full of senses

with the last lovers
we will still be new
the young woman said
fate and death
they are most true

and this is what the angels envy us for
they may have all the life they want
but not all the wants
they could taste

we may be here alone
but we're alone together

HOW WE LIVE

how we live

beating
someone pounding on
wood kicking a door down
splintering

I'm in the bathroom
alone naked
clothes in the hall
but the house is locked

oh the wind
I remember last night
blew down the neighbor's
fence she's beating

nails
into the wood   there
I can hear it
in the trees now

LOST

for Darlene

one   dead white cat
under the shed
you saw it first
see more now
moving slowly on crutches

ghost cat
color of your plaster cast
lying on its side
legs paired
hide buckling over bones

dead a long time
past any smell

gray dust sifted from floor boards
chalk smear
on the shadows in her eye
cat
chose this place to die

maybe hit by a car
headlights swinging
too quickly not stopping
had just enough time
to crawl here

you didn't crawl
anywhere you lay on the hood
against the windshield
your leg howling
louder than sirens

two   rescue crews tell how it happens
after searching for a week
they spot a smudge fire
lost hiker waving them down

helicopter lands in the clearing
they jump out under blade wind
hiker lies down in bent grass
dead before they get there

> *let go too soon*
> *of the long steel wire inside*

> *now I am saved*

gray-blue cat missing for days
he finally heard her cries
in the wall traced them down
to the basement furnace vent

inside   scorched and sooty
nails worn to stubs against the brick
lifted out on his hands she
purred and died

three   when a president dies
            newspaper artists
            airbrush out of the official portrait
            the highlights in the eyes

            even with eyes closed
            flesh speaks of its vacancy
            grandmother in her casket
            sliding off her bones

            cadavers at the medical school
            look smoked   leather eyelids
            mummies in glass cases
            their eyes powder

            but the open look of death

            I found my cat curled up in the weeds
            even before the ants crawled
            out of her mouth
            her stare turned me away

            screaming

(and I love bach's cantatas)

seems like I cry
every day about something
a friend says be careful who you tell that
they might lock you up but
it seems crazy to me
to read through a newsmagazine and not
cry you know what I mean

every year thousands of birds
die in migration
their magnetic navigation messed up by
big TV antennas
their automatic pilots older than the ice age
splatting them up against sky
scrapers in the middle of the night

> we don't need
> skyscrapers or TV
> you could take
> a roll of butcher paper
> and with small letters
> write on both sides
> in narrow columns
> all the things
> we don't need

I don't understand why
we are so different
from everything else I don't know
where we came from why we think
this place is our plaything

we have it coming and I would say fine
except the way it looks now
we'll take all the innocents
with us

      maybe we could build
a big bomb for blowing up
only human beings and our
excrescences I would rather have
the columbia flowing free and clean
than all bach's cantatas

there is no edge to anything

this woman's fingernails
are long and pointed
how can she dig in the earth
without it packing between
the soft flesh and filed shine
so she wears gloves
bends from the waist so her slacks
won't bag and pours
because she wants gravel
and hates to weed
poison
on the ground

we are a complicated tissue of events
we breathe the fumes from that chemical factory
and sometime next month will drink
from the water table underneath her driveway

table bearing our fruits
we who have outsmarted ourselves
and now are full of dread

each breath we take
holds atoms from the mouths of saints
all sighs   cries   bellows   shrieks
every creature blew who did
or will exist the slow

exhale of tides and stars
is this what we want to do
combine them into withering gall
split them open for fire
we are too clever to worship
till our cells run wild

judgment

he had the nerve to come to her funeral
it wasn't a funeral it was a
memorial service
we sat around a candle
at the quaker meeting hall
remembered her to one another
it never occurred to me
he might come

all of a sudden I heard his voice
a razor coated with guile
he was sitting in the midst of us
how did he get there
he was speaking like a mortician
about what he had learned from her
I heard my blood
static in my temples

my blood hot up my arms and legs
I stood up in the room
staring down at him
I heard myself say we know
who killed her
but it was my mind's voice no sound
no one heard words if words were heard
they were of the mind also

I would like to say he stumbled up
and left or we all rose
and he ran for his life
I would like to say

we had her to ourselves again
stood with her in death
would not let him touch her in death
but no one did that
no one saw him run

the beet poem

they were pulling beets
paid in kind

one morning she heard
him in the outhouse
shouting

she opened the door he showed her
paper in his hand: bloody shit

she knelt on the floor
arms around his bare legs
they cried together he sick out of work
no way to pay a doctor

then

they both remembered

the beets

and laughed
laughed themselves giddy
sitting there in the outhouse
noses running

was the best thing happened in months
the high
lasted all day

letter

the greenhouse works fine
mold growing on the walls
velvet gray   brown   soft black
light yellow patches
at first I thought oh
my shiny white walls but
now I stand and look at them
notice where the mold likes
to grow   behind the barrels
or where the rafters meet the roofbeam

Bill who owns the junkyard
salvaged an old oak rocker
out of a demolished hotel
he stripped and oiled it
said it was for the greenhouse
but I couldn't bring myself
to put it there   let it rot
so it's in the bedroom
I figure we can use a chair
for the afternoon sun
or to sit by a sickbed in

then Randy found an oak straightback
at an auction   bought it for the store
but Bernie didn't want it
(I think he saw I liked it)
so he gave it to me
it's missing two braces
three slats out the back
but the arm rests curve gently
and it won't mind the mold

search

he was due home by supper
but I didn't worry till midnight
that's when I called the hospitals
and the highway patrol   at two
I tried the ranger station
nearest that trailhead

        I said no I didn't mind
        being woke up that's my job
        and drove the jeep up to see
        yeah his car was still there
        so I notified the chief
        of the search and rescue crew

           and I phoned her   told her
           look my boys are tired
           we just got in from three days
           risking our necks I'm gonna ask you
           straight did you have a fight
           did he go off to kill himself
           I don't say this to be mean but

that's all right I understand
no we didn't fight like that
he didn't want to die
any more than most of us

           so I got a description
           of him and his gear any medications
           how experienced he was
           and where he was headed
           I said we can't start till
           dawn   that's when we'll roll

I paced a lot and cried some
apologized for everything I ever did
that hurt him promised
never to do it again even prayed

it got light   the day wore on
each time the phone rang
I jumped like it hit me

      it'd be me
      I'd get radio from s & r
      keep her posted how it looked
      I heard them call a copter in
      then cancel it I didn't know
      why   all of a sudden they said
      they had a find

what does that mean they have a find
I saw him at the bottom of a lake
at the bottom of a cliff
broken on rocks

      actually I was at the bottom
      of a stream valley tangled up
      in alder thickets tried first
      crossing cirques but the snow was loose
      it was slow going in the dark

so I slept by the river
hauled ass next morning
two people coming in wondered
was I the one they were looking for
sure enough the parking lot was full
of jeeps and gear I headed over
to the fellow with the walkie talkie
and pulled on his sleeve

coming back from the hospital

where everyone was crisp and white
and cool and efficient

nothing in my stomach since yesterday
except for the strawberry flavored chalk
I saw go down on the x-ray screen

walking toward the bus stop I saw
the bus already leaving   turning
the next corner I decided to run

down the hill across the street
just in front of it in the gutter
spreading my arms like to catch it

but it passed me   stopped
in the next block where one person
got on I held my belly

and sprinted   it waited
I jumped on the first step panted thanks
the black woman driver smiled

apologized she couldn't stop between
signs I said I knew she couldn't my arms
meant the universe is unfair we laughed

I dropped into a seat two old women
sitting ahead of me turned around
one said we saw how far you had to run

we rooted for you

LABORATORY REPORT

FRACTAL SET

response to a theory in mathematics

one   this fall the japanese maple turned coral red
last fall it turned the color of pumpkins
if I were a photographer
I would take a picture at its height each year
when every leaf was done
before a rainstorm blew it into a skeleton

trees turn first in valleys   along creeks
up their streams   fingers
on the hand of a watershed   then
the fire spreads out between those veins
across the map to the ridgetops
up the altitude lines like stairs

if I were a photographer
I would hang out of a small plane each afternoon
take pictures of a stream valley every day through fall
make them frames of a film   watch color move
I would choose one leaf
see every morning after the dew dried
a few more cells turned red or brown

I would take pictures of that leaf   its veins
the same as the valley
run their films side by side on the screen
then pick one frame from each
hang them together on a wall
call it autumn

two   I am in love with the irregular
and unpredictable   what distinguishes
the hand-thrown from machine-stamped pot
forest from tree farm

my life will wander
in its own brownian way I will not
smooth to a clean curve

you will find me between dimensions somewhere
plugging my ears
to the sirens of science and philosophy
who claim to show me what is real and true
arouse me to the brink of mental orgasm

then cheat me
trick me with mind games
word play
only a different way of measuring
the periphery of mystery

I am content with the mystery now

I will accumulate unique particular
and infinitely detailed details
if they suggest a shape by the swarm they make
if they surround or gesture towards
what we can never know

that will suffice
that will be
more than enough

three   rivet fell out of your canvas shoe
metal circle punched through
warp and weft:
                    now that it's gone
you look closely
                  the round hole
squares itself

            difficult to weave a circle
on a square loom: weavers vie
with one another and with the limits
of their craft
                    galleries fill
with woven circles
                      each aspiring
to the bend in the mind's eye
                          corners
hallucinating into arcs

frayed ends of the canvas threads
reach up from the edge of the flat cloth
reach down into the hole

            something moves us
into a new dimension:
                    tears through
grips us with the iron bite of a trap
wears us thin
                and falls away

            a weaver takes scissors
walks up to the loom
snips open a curve

laboratory report

only by reasoning are we able to get
some kind of order into this matter
since we have lost our feeling for it

    —18th century architect

if the nature of the universe is such
that we cannot know the nature of the universe
and any inquiry into apparent regularity or
predictability yeilds unpredictability
irregularity detail window panes becoming
halls of mirrors becoming a kaliedoscope
the presence of the observer altering
the observed every honest answer
a cloud of questions the presence
of the observer ultimately
creating the observed

we are led past tantalizing
conclusions auras of the possibility
of understanding the seeming patterns
themselves a part of the play of randomness
and when the random play has rhythm
repeats itself   makes delicious tension
between unlike forms or otherwise is beautiful
we find significance: truth:
we exult or tremble while it lasts

and time the imaginary succession
close cousin to slow cold entropy saying

all this all this all this all this
is already over you only think
you will your life your life will move
in the same erratic wanderings
as the particle in this glass of water
when the path turns upon itself
when you recognize a shape however brief
you feel the breath of fate
of meaning: you trust   you believe

meanwhile
the lines drawn between
the points of your moving
soon cover the plane

if all this is a trick to dissuade me from
wondering a veil a complex withdrawal
down the corridor ahead of me dense mists
of silent probabilities politely but firmly
refusing to be firm

or if it is in fact the way it is

either way I step back out
of the gray and black and white
of electron microscopes radio telescopes
into the band of color again

I know the spoon does not bend in the glass
but I will wrap my hand around them

I will come to my senses the rushing of fire
in this wood stove the particular
irregular unpredictable rufous-sided towhee
pecking millet outside this window
this hearbeat I feel in my temple
and the next one these
are my comfort and sanity
all I want all I need
to know

the healer

leaning backwards into the wind of
future blowing leaves past sides of sight
looking ahead back down corridor
tunnel sucking leaves gold specks
pulsing under pressed eyelids

to stay in the moment
is to beat frail feathers
against earthpull deathpull
but it can

       open into a desert landscape
unrolling with the bang of sets
light inhaled away by the first stars
out of the ancient fireball escaping
everywhere sudden chord of a total
eclipse corona writhing
the spheres
hanging

      in a room so close we don't
see it looking out
into each other's windows
when we reach for the metal doorknob
we tap it first for shock

                    each
second our circuits retrieve
all the available data similar
to the situation we're strategy animals
we grieve rage joy mostly memory
already nostalgic for the present

but the fork in the road is a delta now
the channels shifting

amor fati

they free themselves from unnecessary decisions
from fashion material status separate tactfully
from the expectations of their families
they work for a living occasional wages
suffice for food and clothing a room
they claim no direction
no goal

some feel in their bones ancestral marrow
an old country cast of countenance
some remember the surround
of former flesh have more in common
with fate than with kin
the river steps down into pools revolves
first cell to the universe:
just teach me how to stay alive
I can take care of the rest myself

where does it belong the knowing
riding over the wall in a surge of pain
a stab of light or a sliding out the tunnel
into nakedness and blood
the floor of the abyss is splitting apart
the land moves whole continents drift
from pole to equator the history of the world
is not what it seemed truth
is not enough

        blood is a stubborn stain
it refuses to allow us to forget

we're all related red blood
or the amber blood of bees
tree blood clear as water we came from
some carry inside others float in
water the celestials envy us for
none anywhere else

                        the structure of embrace
turns what we must love into what we
can love a short cut to sanity
to live outside the law you must be honest
said the singer who later gave up
and found five octaves above high C
is the color green three below the lowest key
is my hand waving

the candle flame dims it says
now comes the darkness
it has never known darkness because it is light
but it says I am going to die
darkness is descending closing in
I feel it nudging and stroking me
now I am dying now it will be dark
the wick glows red wisp of smoke
rises gray against shadows
and then it is dark

LIGHTNING NEAR THE TOWER

In contrast to the feminine mysteries,
the transformation mysteries of the Archetypal Masculine
have the character of a surprise attack,
and sudden eruptions are the decisive factor.
Consequently, lightning is the characteristic symbol for them.

Erich Neumann, The Great Mother

. . . supreme moment at which one arrives in the full light
of day, but a moment surrounded by a ring of darkness.
For it is not without danger that one lifts oneself
to the summits of the mind.

George Poulet, "The Dream of Descartes"
from Studies in Human Time

THE BEAST

there is infinite hope,
but not for us.

Franz Kafka

I can't help it
this morning walking down the bus
to a seat all the faces
dozing looking out at the rain
trusting   I loved them
I wanted to say out loud we're doomed
we're all doomed

empty office before eight
no one else there I saw it
splintered plaster crumpled glass
flashing in when I was small
we were taught to crawl under desks
away from windows

riding my bike I think
this must be like the early christians
the lord is at hand
why begin anything
since high school the book on hiroshima
hand of god anytime anywhere
is this what I want to be found doing
will it happen now

the hot sword flay me

churchill called it the second coming
in wrath that july dawn
when a ranchwoman in new mexico
saw the sun rise twice

they telegraphed truman in potsdam
scientists who made it
said *the baby is born you could have heard*
his screams from here to the farm

small town of belen little bethlehem
they call it eighty miles north
of ground zero the valley *conquistadores*
named *jornada del muerto*
in a ring of precambrian mountains
from before life no fossils in them
no sign

it's terrible after we made love
last night falling asleep together
under flannel sheets I felt
slap of fire slash my windows
and we lay scalded
bursting water and blood

the tower

. . . the frog-shaped Heqet . . . primordial mother
of all existence, which she generates and
protects.

Erich Neumann, The Great Mother

toads called spadefoot survived
slow drying of the southwest sea
now new mexico learned to dig
sometimes fifteen feet down stay
weeks at a time

        once a road crew found
under old concrete in a baked clay ball
one of them still alive

        eyes cat slits
they surface to eat only at night
instead of breeding in spring they mate
whenever it rains

        night before trinity
what oppenheimer named first
bomb test after donne's holy sonnet
batter my heart three person'd god
thunderstorm over ground zero

lightning near the tower

before dawn
in the bunkers six miles away they heard
spadefoot song loudest among toads and frogs
hurry I've found water to mate in

hundreds moving mounting leaving
moonstone clouds on the sand wet
still enough for tadpoles maybe
long enough for them to turn

sunrise man announcing countdown
loudspeakers over trenches wondered
microphone in his hand *would it*
somewhere between five and four
electrocute him if he held it spoke
ONE threw it to the floor screamed

ZERO

between his scream and the bloom of death
only sound was the toads' singing

to command a good view

the streams and the rocks there
were mysteriously elegant.
now everything is turned to ashes.

   Fujiwara Munetada
   The Chuyuki (A.D. 1093)

a.   kyoto, 1090:

the emperor asked the old gardener
to name for him the most outstanding
among the famous gardens of the time

the old man   son of a chief steward
author of a treatise on garden making
known as a master of this devotion
answered first a renowned villa
second his late father's former home

the real reason the emperor asked
was that he himself had designed a garden
and expected to hear it named   he said
the third one must surely be the palace

but the old man replied *oh yes of course*
your majesty supervised its making
but the view there is quite ordinary
I regret to say the third choice must be
the garden of my own pavilion

toward the close of three years later
the old gardener's house was torched

and the garden burned to the ground with it
seriously ill he renounced the world
found refuge and death in a monastery

the emperor claimed the charred field
and built a palace there

b.   seattle, 1982:

saturday during the heat wave
I watered shrubs
bending among them with hoses
to keep them alive
my arms legs face
covered against burn so hot
every half hour I limped inside
for juice and shade

I wondered how much greater would a fireball be
all the leaves and trees I can see made dead
dead and powder on a gray plain

I said that night
when we turned to talk together after the speaker
and a nurse insisted on survivors the will to live
I would be useless I would be paralyzed by grief

now on a rainy evening
walking barefoot

over cool wet flagstones
in a soft kimono
I am mystified we have come to this
we will suck loveliness
into wind sand bone
to prove we are strong

c. _____, _____:

(this hasn't been written yet, it has to do
with losing everything loved and familiar and possible
all at once so quickly you would go mad

except for the fires the dust the shattered glass
in your boiled arm how thirsty you've become
piles of ash and rubble as far as you can see

a great quiet and nothing around moving
this is the meaning of the tree of knowledge
the burning sword and banishment

except there is no angel
and no place to go)

homana

oh for a heart as pure
as pollen on corn blossoms

Polingaysi Qoyawayma
No Turning Back

the hopi spokeswoman over the telephone
speaks to me low and slowly of prophecy
how a gourd of ashes will drop from the sky
a tower of ashes like a mushroom
and the earth be consumed in flame
how the signs we are past turning back
will be a ladder to the moon a volcano
great disasters in strange places famine
and the wuwuchim kachina
dancing in the plaza

the last time the wuwuchim kachina danced
fifty years ago it carried a rattle
on one side painted a swastika
on the other a rising sun

the earth whom sound and light made spins
on her backbone sings like rushing of wind
finds balance from rock the light-skinned ones
as was foretold have dug and crushed
for power which badly used
makes a weapon to kill

this is all ordained but not predestined
we are given choice and the will to choose

but the time has come to live with effort

she is in the city to say farewell
to a dying friend who regrets to leave
because he has met a woman he loves
she says I may write these things they are
not only about hopi when I write
they will gather around my shoulders
I will know I have permission
by how the words come

                she says *I have heard*
from the holy man at hotevilla he told me
the wuwuchim kachina
has danced again in the plaza

angelus

the evening bell

mother of mercy
ever bearing fleece of prophecy
who one night attracted the dew
everything else dry
and the next night mild smooth wool
stayed dry yourself in the rain

rain your milk clear and pure
over rocks at timberline
or rich with loam broth and sun
swinging around the last curve
to the ocean

       ancient star of the sea
arcing over our shipdeck
water star heaving and shining under us
as we all lean away from the light

give us of that mercy
you carry in your strong arms
tonight's fir trees swaying
branches heavy with early pollen
promise of storm on the wind at dusk

hold us hard and tightly
let us cry out the tiredness

of this day's work of good and evil
swing us high till we thrill
with safety laughter tremble

enough so we can fall asleep now
enough to embrace the morning

Cover painting: *The Benefactor / Daylight Angel* by Linda Okazaki
photograph by Paul Boyer

Typography: Graphiti, Port Townsend, WA

154   900

Desire